MY WASHINGTON, DC

Kathy Jakobsen

LB

LITTLE, BROWN AND COMPANY

New York   Boston

My name is Becky, and last weekend my best friend Martin and I took the train to Washington, DC. My mother painted me a map before we went—you can see it in the front of this book. We always have contests on trips. The Washington contest was to find eagles and stars. See how many you can count in my mother's paintings—some of them

are really hard to see! The Washington train station was huge and really fancy; it has a marble floor, and the designs on the ceiling are made with over seventy pounds of gold! Martin and I noticed that Union Station is just a short walk from Capitol Hill, so we decided to go there next.

We walked up Capitol Hill—which really is a hill—through a shady park, and headed to the visitor center. All around us were marble buildings: the Capitol, the Supreme Court, and the Library of Congress. It was easy to imagine the buildings when they were first built, white and sparkling and new, planned to be worthy of the first government in the world that was a republic of the people, by the people, and for the people.

After the American Revolution, George Washington picked out land where the capital city would be. Washington approved the design for the Capitol Building, too, and praised it for being grand, convenient, and simple all at once. He put in the first stone himself. In the visitor center we saw the plaster version of the nineteen-and-a-half-foot-tall Statue of Freedom. We thought she looked fierce with her eagle headdress.

My favorite part of the Capitol was National Statuary Hall on the second floor, because there's a "whispering gallery." Plaques in the floor show where famous people sat in the old days when the House of Representatives met there. I found the plaque for John Quincy Adams. The legend goes that he used to

sit there, pretending to be asleep—but really he was listening to his enemies talking at the other end of the hall! They didn't know that he could hear them. If you want to try it, stand near where his desk used to be while friends talk (or even whisper!) at the other end of the room.

I was really excited to visit the Library of Congress. It not only contains books but also hundreds of interesting collections. There are recordings of everything you can think of, from folk songs by famous singers like Woody Guthrie to American Indian songs and stories (in their tribal languages) to a collection of jump-rope songs by sixth-grade girls at a

Washington, DC, school. They are part of the Archive of Folk Culture, which collects traditions from around the world. The Library of Congress also includes historical collections, such as all the things that were in President Abraham Lincoln's pockets the night he was shot. Even the building itself is interesting—I walked right into Martin because I was so busy looking at the artwork on the ceiling!

When the nine Supreme Court justices get to work, they always shake hands with one another. It helps them stay polite and friendly, even when they are debating. Any American has the right to challenge any law. Some cases go through the legal system all the way to the Supreme Court. Then the justices must decide whether the law is constitutional. Martin and I agree with the carving on the building that says *EQUAL JUSTICE UNDER LAW*.

At the National Archives, we saw the Declaration of Independence, which declared that the Colonies were no longer going to be ruled by King George III and the English Parliament. The ink letters are really faded, and at first that was disappointing. But then we saw the name Matthew Thornton. I'm related to him! Some people in our family are always late and we joke that he must have been late for the signing, because his signature is the very last one.

THE BILL of RIGHTS

AMENDMENT I
CONGRESS SHALL MAKE NO LAW RESPECTING AN ESTABLISHMENT OF RELIGION, OR PROHIBITING THE FREE EXERCISE THEREOF; OR ABRIDGING THE FREEDOM OF SPEECH, OR OF THE PRESS; OR THE RIGHT OF THE PEOPLE PEACEABLY TO ASSEMBLE, AND TO PETITION THE GOVERNMENT FOR A REDRESS OF GRIEVANCES.

AMENDMENT II
A WELL REGULATED MILITIA, BEING NECESSARY TO THE SECURITY OF A FREE STATE, THE RIGHT OF THE PEOPLE TO KEEP AND BEAR ARMS, SHALL NOT BE INFRINGED.

AMENDMENT III
NO SOLDIER SHALL, IN TIME OF PEACE BE QUARTERED IN ANY HOUSE, WITHOUT THE CONSENT OF THE OWNER, NOR IN TIME OF WAR, BUT IN A MANNER TO BE PRESCRIBED BY LAW.

AMENDMENT IV
THE RIGHT OF THE PEOPLE TO BE SECURE IN THEIR PERSONS, HOUSES, PAPERS, AND EFFECTS, AGAINST UNREASONABLE SEARCHES AND SEIZURES, SHALL NOT BE VIOLATED, AND NO WARRANTS SHALL ISSUE, BUT UPON PROBABLE CAUSE, SUPPORTED BY OATH OR AFFIRMATION, AND PARTICULARLY DESCRIBING THE PLACE TO BE SEARCHED, AND THE PERSONS OR THINGS TO BE SEIZED.

AMENDMENT V
NO PERSON SHALL BE HELD TO ANSWER FOR A CAPITAL, OR OTHERWISE INFAMOUS CRIME, UNLESS ON A PRESENTMENT OR INDICTMENT OF A GRAND JURY, EXCEPT IN CASES ARISING IN THE LAND OR NAVAL FORCES, OR IN THE MILITIA, WHEN IN ACTUAL SERVICE IN TIME OF WAR OR PUBLIC DANGER; NOR SHALL ANY PERSON BE SUBJECT FOR THE SAME OFFENSE TO BE TWICE PUT IN JEOPARDY OF LIFE OR LIMB; NOR SHALL BE COMPELLED IN ANY CRIMINAL CASE TO BE A WITNESS AGAINST HIMSELF, NOR BE DEPRIVED OF LIFE, LIBERTY, OR PROPERTY, WITHOUT DUE PROCESS OF LAW; NOR

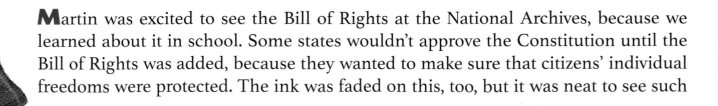

Martin was excited to see the Bill of Rights at the National Archives, because we learned about it in school. Some states wouldn't approve the Constitution until the Bill of Rights was added, because they wanted to make sure that citizens' individual freedoms were protected. The ink was faded on this, too, but it was neat to see such

THE FIRST TEN AMENDMENTS TO THE CONSTITUTION *of* THE UNITED STATES *of* AMERICA

SHALL PRIVATE PROPERTY BE TAKEN FOR PUBLIC USE, WITHOUT JUST COMPENSATION.

AMENDMENT VI IN ALL CRIMINAL PROSECUTIONS, THE ACCUSED SHALL ENJOY THE RIGHT TO A SPEEDY AND PUBLIC TRIAL, BY AN IMPARTIAL JURY OF THE STATE AND DISTRICT WHEREIN THE CRIME SHALL HAVE BEEN COMMITTED, WHICH DISTRICT SHALL HAVE BEEN PREVIOUSLY ASCERTAINED BY LAW, AND TO BE INFORMED OF THE NATURE AND CAUSE OF THE ACCUSATION; TO BE CONFRONTED WITH THE WITNESSES AGAINST HIM; TO HAVE COMPULSORY PROCESS FOR OBTAINING WITNESSES IN HIS FAVOR, AND TO HAVE THE ASSISTANCE OF COUNSEL FOR HIS DEFENSE.

AMENDMENT VII IN SUITS AT COMMON LAW, WHERE THE VALUE IN CONTROVERSY SHALL EXCEED TWENTY DOLLARS, THE RIGHT OF TRIAL BY JURY SHALL BE PRESERVED, AND NO FACT TRIED BY A JURY, SHALL BE OTHERWISE RE-EXAMINED IN ANY COURT OF THE UNITED STATES, THAN ACCORDING TO THE RULES OF THE COMMON LAW.

AMENDMENT VIII EXCESSIVE BAIL SHALL NOT BE REQUIRED, NOR EXCESSIVE FINES IMPOSED, NOR CRUEL AND UNUSUAL PUNISHMENTS INFLICTED.

AMENDMENT IX THE ENUMERATION IN THE CONSTITUTION, OF CERTAIN RIGHTS, SHALL NOT BE CONSTRUED TO DENY OR DISPARAGE OTHERS RETAINED BY THE PEOPLE.

AMENDMENT X THE POWERS NOT DELEGATED TO THE UNITED STATES BY THE CONSTITUTION, NOR PROHIBITED BY IT TO THE STATES, ARE RESERVED TO THE STATES RESPECTIVELY, OR TO THE PEOPLE.

RATIFIED DECEMBER 15th 1791

an important piece of history. My mother painted us a new version so we could read every word—we had to look up a lot of them! We learned that after the Bill of Rights was agreed on, fourteen copies were made: one to be kept by the government, and the other thirteen to be kept by each of the original colonies.

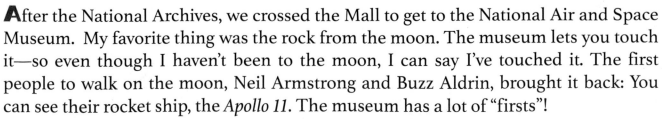

After the National Archives, we crossed the Mall to get to the National Air and Space Museum. My favorite thing was the rock from the moon. The museum lets you touch it—so even though I haven't been to the moon, I can say I've touched it. The first people to walk on the moon, Neil Armstrong and Buzz Aldrin, brought it back: You can see their rocket ship, the *Apollo 11*. The museum has a lot of "firsts"!

When you go into the National Museum of Natural History, you see a huge African elephant. They also have the famous blue Hope Diamond, which was bought by an American heiress named Evalyn Walsh McLean in 1911. She wore it to fancy parties, but she also put it on her dog and hid it in her toaster. When she went to a hospital to visit sick soldiers, she let them throw it from bed to bed. She even wore it on a roller coaster!

We finally reached the White House! George Washington chose this building's design, but it was called the President's House then. The next president, John Adams, and his wife, Abigail, moved in before the building was completely finished ("Shiver, shiver!" Abigail wrote to her daughter, referring to the cold house), and all the presidents since have lived there. We found out about a lot of animals that have been presidential

pets or passed through the White House! President Lincoln's son Tad hitched his pet goat to a kitchen chair and drove it through a party his mother was hosting in the East Room. One of Theodore Roosevelt's sons brought his pony Algonquin upstairs in the elevator to cheer up his sick brother. Imagine what a wreck the White House would be if all these animals were inside at the same time!

OVAL
OFFICE

A lot of kids have lived in the White House. All six of Theodore Roosevelt's children roller-skated in the East Room. Tad Lincoln and his brother fired a toy cannon at the Cabinet Room while the Cabinet was meeting. There is a bowling alley at the White House, along with a movie theater and

EXECUTE THE OFFICE OF PRESIDENT OF THE UNITED STATES, DEFEND THE CONSTITUTION OF THE UNITED STATES."

ARTICLE II SECTION I OF THE UNITED STATES CONSTITUTION

a putting green! Of course, most of the building is used by the president to live and do his job—Martin and I got to see the Oval Office, where the president works. It's in the West Wing of the White House so the president can go back and forth between his home and office quickly.

Lightbulb (1879)

Original Kodak camera (1888)

Cast-iron toy fire engine (c. 1900)

Crayola crayons (1903)

Babe Ruth signed baseball (c. 1926)

Remington typewriter (1874)

Double eagle gold coin (1933)

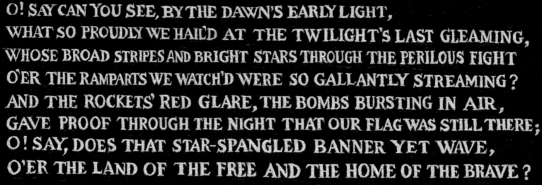

O! SAY CAN YOU SEE, BY THE DAWN'S EARLY LIGHT,
WHAT SO PROUDLY WE HAIL'D AT THE TWILIGHT'S LAST GLEAMING,
WHOSE BROAD STRIPES AND BRIGHT STARS THROUGH THE PERILOUS FIGHT
O'ER THE RAMPARTS WE WATCH'D WERE SO GALLANTLY STREAMING?
AND THE ROCKETS' RED GLARE, THE BOMBS BURSTING IN AIR,
GAVE PROOF THROUGH THE NIGHT THAT OUR FLAG WAS STILL THERE;
O! SAY, DOES THAT STAR-SPANGLED BANNER YET WAVE,
O'ER THE LAND OF THE FREE AND THE HOME OF THE BRAVE?

Abraham Lincoln's top hat (1865)

The Wizard of Oz ruby slippers (1939)

Benjamin Franklin's three-piece suit (1778)

Hershey's Tropical Chocolate Bar (1943)

Thomas Jefferson's desk (1776)

Howdy Doody puppet (1949)

Teapot (1766–70)

Sony "Walkman" Cassette Player (c. 1980)

Teddy bear (1903)

After we visited the White House, we walked back to the National Museum of American History, which had lots of interesting objects from our country's past. It has the actual flag that flew over the fort they sang about in "The Star-Spangled Banner." It's tattered. Martin thought it might be from "the bombs bursting in air," but it's because the family that owned the flag gave away snippets as souvenirs! I was amazed at how big it was. It's the size of the wall!

"...I HAVE A DREAM THAT MY FOUR LITTLE CHILDREN WILL ONE DAY LIVE IN A NATION WHERE THEY WILL NOT BE JUDGED BY THE COLOR OF THEIR SKIN BUT BY THE CONTENT OF THEIR CHARACTER...."

In the 1950s and '60s, Dr. Martin Luther King Jr. inspired the country to support laws that give all Americans the same rights. Hundreds of thousands of people marched from the Washington Monument to the Lincoln Memorial and heard him deliver his famous "I Have a Dream" speech. His statue is carved into the "Stone of Hope," and it stands in front of the "Mountain of Despair." These names come from his "I Have a Dream" speech: "Out of the mountain of despair, a stone of hope."

I HAVE SWORN UPON THE ALTAR OF GOD ETERNAL HOSTILITY AG

As we walked around the Tidal Basin, we arrived at the Thomas Jefferson Memorial. Thomas Jefferson wrote the Declaration of Independence, was president, and invented lots of things, including a spaghetti maker and an automatic door. He was also a talented architect, scientist, and gardener. He and John Adams were the only presidents who signed the Declaration of Independence, and they both died on its fiftieth anniversary on the Fourth of July in 1826.

When Congress decided to build a memorial for Jefferson, they modeled it on a building that had inspired Jefferson himself: the Pantheon in Rome. To spell out Jefferson's hopes for this country, parts of the Declaration of Independence are inscribed on one of the building's walls. I loved seeing the cherry blossoms in bloom! The trees were a gift from Japan, and you can see the flowers every year at the National Cherry Blossom Festival.

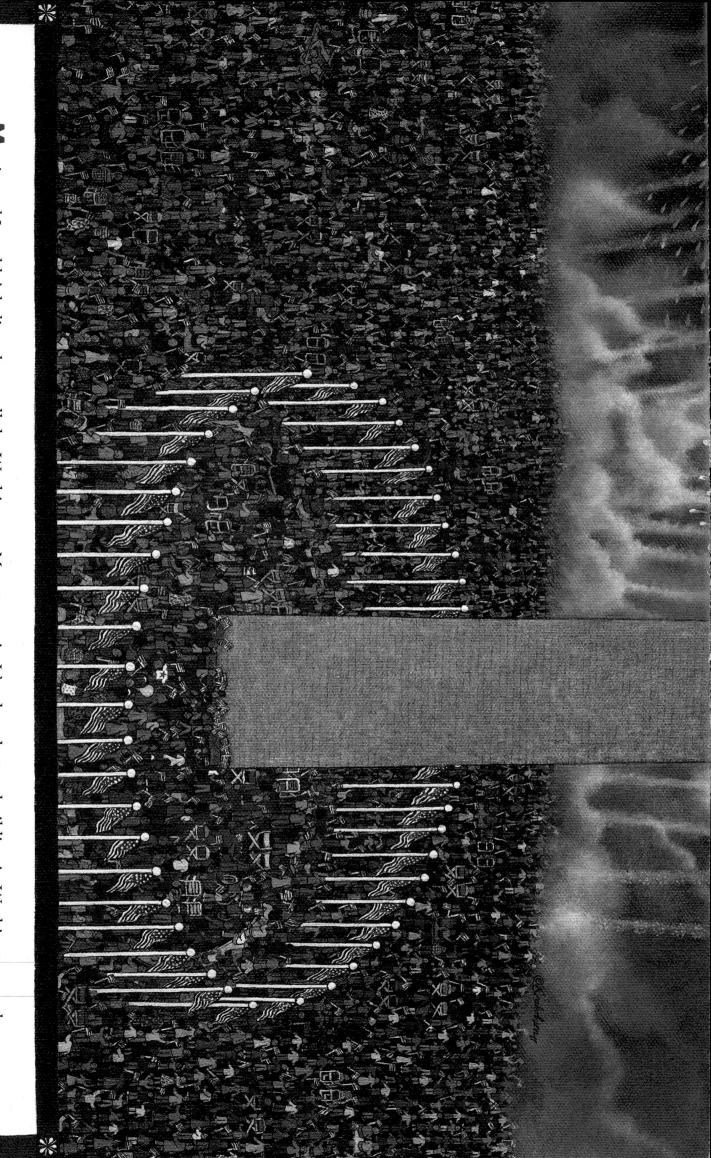

Martin and I couldn't believe how tall the Washington Monument is. It's a law that no building in Washington can be taller than the Capitol Building, except the Washington Monument. Martin knew that this type of monument was called an obelisk and told me that it's the tallest obelisk in the world. We thought it was a tribute to Washington, DC, but found out it was built in honor of George Washington. We had fun counting all fifty flags around the base—one for every state!

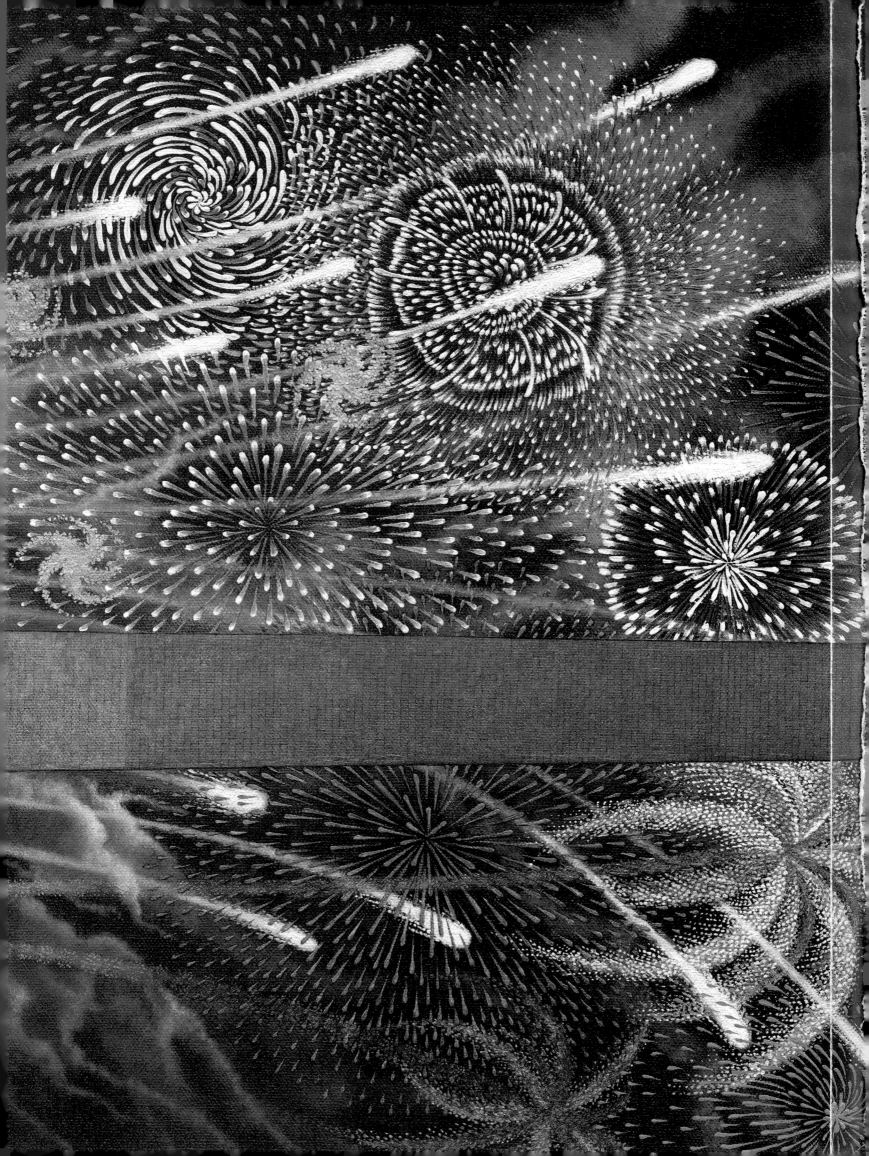

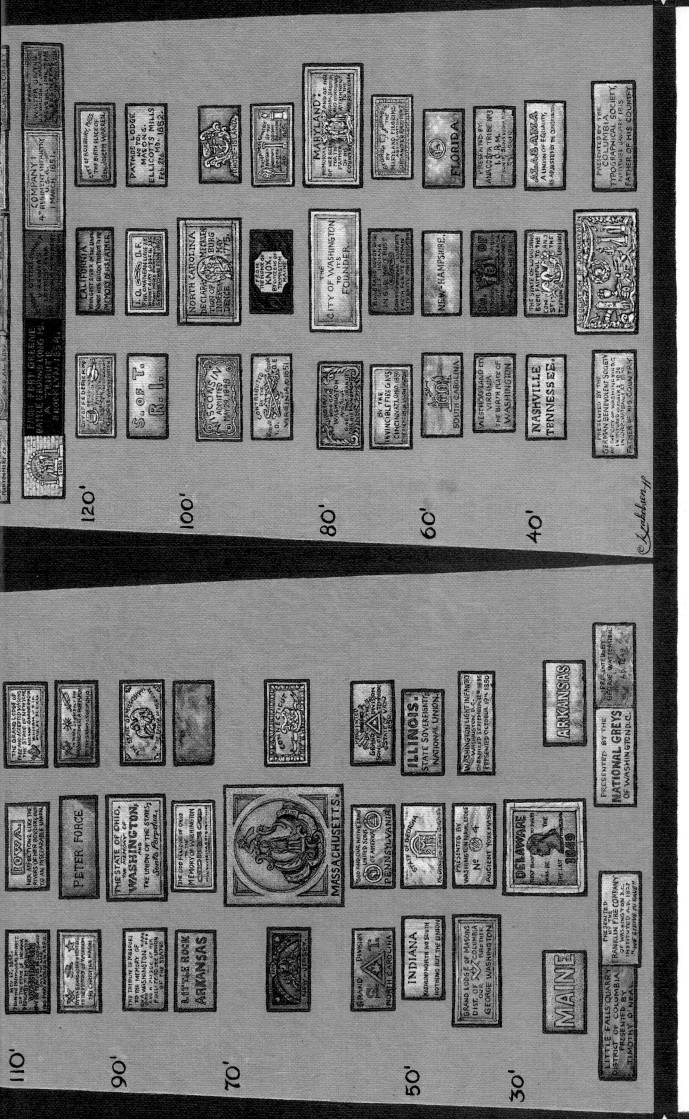

We learned that the Washington National Monument Society ran out of money long before the building was finished, and they asked all the schoolchildren in America to "give a penny" so this monument could be completed. The society also asked each state to contribute stones. Alabama sent a huge block of marble that was four feet long and two feet high—and soon 192 others sent stones, too: states, American Indian tribes, clubs, foreign countries, even a Boy Scout troop! There is a stone for every state. All of them were inscribed, sometimes with the group's name, sometimes just with a message or a date.

We could see the Lincoln Memorial from the Washington Monument and went there next. Soon after Abraham Lincoln was elected president, some southern states seceded from the Union. Lincoln believed that it was his job as president to preserve the Union, so he called for soldiers and the Civil War began. By the time it ended, Lincoln had freed the slaves. Martin and I read the Gettysburg Address, which is a speech Lincoln gave during the Civil War and is carved near his statue.

Dr. King gave his "I Have a Dream" speech on the steps of this memorial, and we can see why. The Lincoln Memorial is a tribute to the man who worked hard so "that government of the people, by the people, for the people shall not perish from the earth." It was the perfect end for a trip to such an important city. I can't believe how much we saw! Now you've seen *my* Washington, DC. Use the map and have fun exploring *your* Washington, DC!

Fun Facts About Washington, DC
Plus a Reader's Challenge

Here are some of my favorite Washington, DC, details. I challenge you to find them in the book's paintings. And I'm sure you noticed Speedy the cat in some paintings, but maybe you didn't know that he is in every one. See if you can spot him! Did you count at least forty eagles and three hundred stars? Martin says he found lots more—see how many you can find!

Union Station
This clock has an unusual trait: Its numbers are written in roman numerals, and normally "4" written in roman numerals is "IV," but on this clock, it's written as "IIII."

Capitol Hill
The woman in this sculpture is holding a copy of the Constitution.

Statuary Hall
Every state was asked to send two statues to display in Statuary Hall, but when they all arrived, it turned out they were too heavy for the room—the floor would have broken under their weight!

Library of Congress
The Library of Congress is the largest library in the world. It contains more than 160 million items and keeps growing every day.

Supreme Court
Supreme Court justices keep their jobs for as long as they want to—even for their entire lives!—unless they do something unlawful or unethical and are impeached.

National Archives
Besides the Declaration of Independence, the National Archives Museum houses the Emancipation Proclamation, the Constitution, and the 1297 Magna Carta.

Bill of Rights
This sun was on the chair George Washington sat in during the Constitutional Convention, which is when the US Constitution was written. The chair is on display in Philadelphia—maybe Martin and I will have to go there next!

National Air and Space Museum
Sputnik 1 was the first artificial satellite to be launched. Its successful launch by the Soviet Union in 1957 began the space age.

National Museum of Natural History

The elephant in the National Museum of Natural History is named Henry.

White House

Three separate US presidents had alligators in the White House: John Quincy Adams, Herbert Hoover, and Benjamin Harrison!

White House

The British burned the President's House during the War of 1812 while James Madison was president. His wife, Dolley, saved George Washington's portrait. After the fire, the house was painted white and people started calling it the White House. That name was officially adopted in 1901.

National Museum of American History

This chocolate bar was specially designed to be used by the US armed forces.

MLK Memorial

The statue of Martin Luther King Jr. is thirty feet tall, compared to the statue of Lincoln in the Lincoln Memorial, which is only nineteen feet tall—though of course, he's sitting down.

Jefferson Memorial

One cherry tree always blooms about a week before all the other trees. The National Park Service uses that "indicator tree" to tell when the cherry blossoms will bloom.

Washington Monument

The tip of the Washington Monument is made out of aluminum. A famous jewelry store in New York City, Tiffany's, displayed the tip in 1884. As the New York Times reported, it was visited by "thousands of New Yorkers who delighted in being able to later say 'I stepped over the top of the Washington Monument.'"

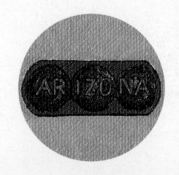

Washington Monument

Most stones that were donated to the Washington Monument were made out of limestone or granite, but some were made out of unusual materials: The stone that Arizona donated was made out of petrified wood.

Lincoln Memorial

There are eighty-seven steps leading up to the Lincoln Memorial—or as you might call them, "four score and seven" steps. You can see names of the states written on the memorial, but my mother ran out of room. Look at a photograph of the memorial and see which state she left out!

Lincoln Memorial

This symbol is called a fasces. For an extra challenge, see how many you can find in My Washington, DC.

Our Founding Fathers had lots of good advice for young people— here are two of my favorite quotes from Thomas Jefferson:

"If ever you are about to say any thing amiss or to do any thing wrong, consider before hand. You will feel something within you which will tell you it is wrong and ought not to be said or done: this is your conscience . . ."
—from a letter to his daughter Martha Jefferson, December 11, 1783

"Whenever you are to do a thing, though it can never be known but to yourself, ask yourself how you would act were all the world looking at you, and act accordingly. Encourage all your virtuous dispositions. . . . It is of great importance to set a resolution, not to be shaken, never to tell an untruth. . . . and he who permits himself to tell a lie once, finds it much easier to do it a second and third time, till at length it becomes habitual; he tells lies without attending to it, and truths without the world's believing him."
—from a letter to his nephew Peter Carr, August 19, 1785

Fun Websites and Songs

What would your life be like if you lived at the White House? This website shows you, with pictures and stories about real kids who have lived there:
www.whitehousehistory.org/teacher-resources/first-kids

We didn't get to see this, but the website is good: You can play spy games and test your spy skills:
www.spymuseum.org/education-programs/kids-families/kidspy-zone

If you're going to the Supreme Court and want to see cases being brought to the justices, this website tells how: *www.supremecourt.gov*

If you want to learn more about some of the places we visited, you can go here: *www.si.edu*

Schoolhouse Rock! is a series of cartoons that include songs about the first words of the Constitution and how a bill becomes a law. You can find these online or at your local library. Some of my favorite songs are "I'm Just a Bill" and "Three Ring Government."

Also Illustrated by Kathy Jakobsen:

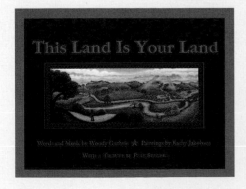
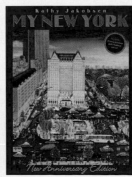
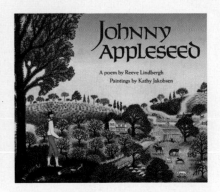

Artist's Note

These paintings were done in oil on canvas, with small amounts of ink, and acrylic gold for the gold-leaf highlights. I use Winsor & Newton Series 7 sable brushes, and make good use of their smallest size, 000. I also use some old, worn-out brushes with only one hair left.

I paint in layers, beginning with large blocks of color, and when those are dry, I put in the buildings and the people. If, for example, I want a bright red color (like Martin's T-shirt), I will paint a white undercoat first, and when that is dry, I paint the red on top of it. The white undercoat makes the color brighter and cleaner. It usually takes several layers to get the color I want. Then, when the colors are right, I will go back and do shading. I often use several transparent glazes to get the subtle colors I want, like in the sky or in the clouds.

My first visit to Washington, DC, was on my high school senior trip. I have also been there with my parents, and as a parent myself with my three children. During the Reagan administration, I was selected to paint the official "Easter at the White House" painting, and visited the White House twice—once to attend the event for research and once to present the finished oil painting. It has been a wonderful adventure exploring Washington, DC, through these paintings. I have tried to be as accurate and detailed as possible—I only wish I could have included more! It is my hope that this book will inspire readers to learn more about the capital city, and about the man who was so instrumental in its founding and for which it was named, George Washington. I hope you enjoy exploring Washington, DC, with Becky, Martin, and Speedy, the orange-and-white cat!

—*Kathy Jakobsen*

Dedicated to Keith, Elizabeth, Martin, and Alana,
and to the Founders and the Constitution that they created
— KJ

Acknowledgments

Special thanks to:

Megan Tingley, Bethany Strout, Connie Hsu, Deirdre Jones, Libby Koponen, Annie McDonnell, Patti Ann Harris, Saho Fujii, Phil Caminiti, Jen Keenan, Maeve Norton, and Erika Schwartz.

Lee and Karen and Bonnie for their support, without which I could not have done this book.

The Smithsonian Institution, Allison Dixon at the National Park Service, staff at the Washington Monument, and Jennifer Vilaga.

My family for their patience and support while I was doing this book!

Remembrance and thanks to the late Edmund Bott, Bob Bishop, and Jay Johnson.

Thanks also to everyone who helped—you know who you are!

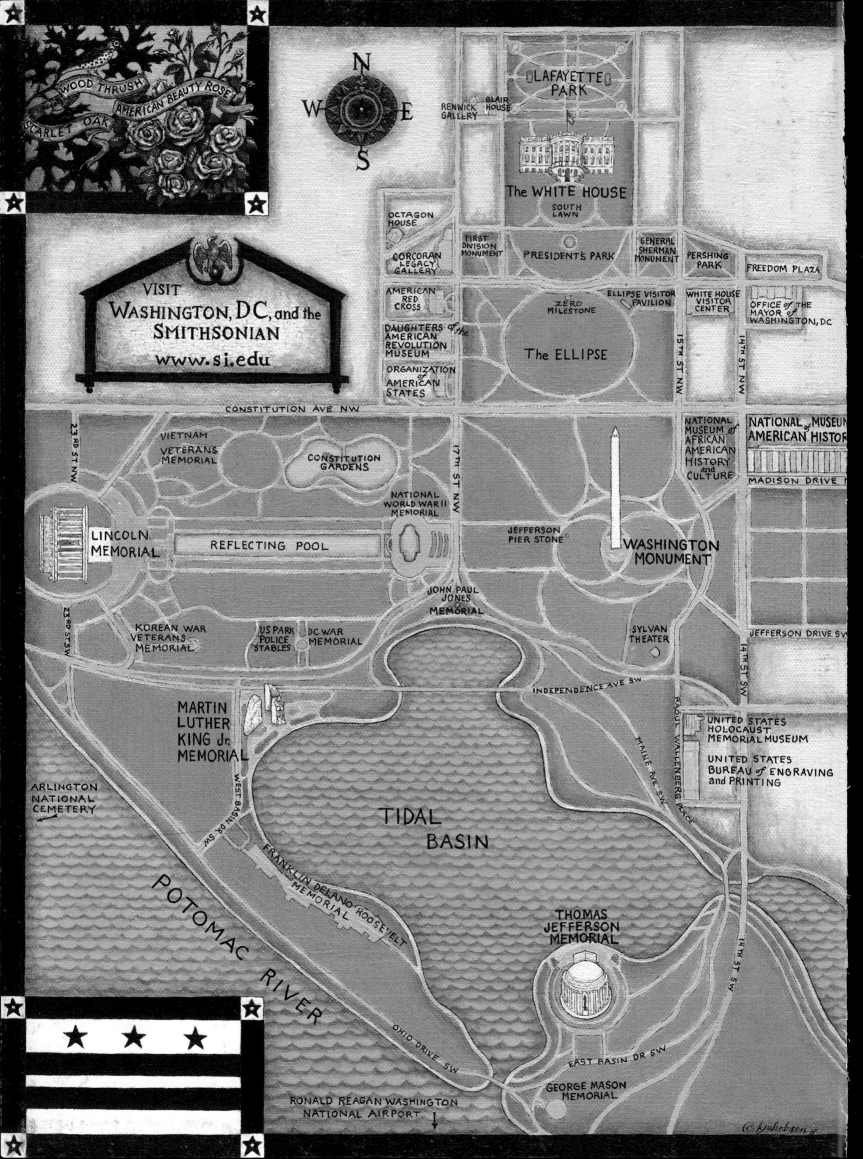